The Forgiveness Fallacies

What Forgiveness is & What it's not!

Pastor Joel L. Rissinger, MA, MRE

8/5/2018

Pastor Joel, in his new excellent essay on the fallacies of forgiveness, walks the reader through just about every preconceived notion we've held concerning this most important subject. I found his 'divine insights' to be honest, true and refreshing. Anyone who has struggled with desiring to know what biblical forgiveness is and isn't will find themselves revisiting this book time and time again.

— Rev. Al Stewart, Author & Senior Pastor, Greater Grace Chapel, Lynchburg, Va.

The prayer Jesus taught the disciples connects God's forgiveness of our sins, to our forgiveness of others (Matthew 6:12). Throughout my 50 years in ministry as a pastor and the director of a Rescue Mission, I have witnessed people defeated by their ignorance and/or rebellion concerning forgiveness. I have also witnessed life-changing victories when people give and receive forgiveness.

Joel has provided a desperately needed tool to help understand how simple and easy it is to forgive and be forgiven. Our enemy has deceived us into a place where we say, I can't (or won't) and God has used Joel to teach us we can. Thank you Joel, for helping us to forgive.

--Pastor Terry Wilcox, Executive Director of Bridgeport Rescue Mission, Bridgeport, CT

"As a Pastor and Counselor of couples and individuals for many years, I have found that many of the problems in the Church and in relationships are mostly due to lack of forgiveness. I have found that almost all problems between people are perpetuated by unforgiveness. Joel has blessed us with a very in-depth and easy to understand book on why forgiveness is so important in our lives. This book can be read in a short amount of time but can change your life. Thank you Joel for your 'direct to the point' writing style and the biblical understanding that you have given to us."

- Pastor Roger Bolduk - Pastor Chaplin Church Chaplin CT, Co-founder Council for Christian Arts, Co-host - In His Presence Radio Network, Board of Directors, Caring Families Pregnancy Center.

"The Forgiveness Fallacies" hits the mark! With wit, clarity, and valuable insight gleamed from over 25 years of ministry, Pastor Joel Rissinger handles the often confused and challenging subject of forgiveness. Read this book, put it into practice and YOU WILL experience the wonderful freedom that only forgiveness brings.

-Stephen A. Cianci, Lead Pastor, LifeWaych.com

"As a Pastor's wife who has been involved in over 25 years of pastoral counseling, I have seen unforgiveness to be one of the greatest stressors across lives and generations. This book provides straightforward direction about what forgiveness is not and what it is. It will help you forgive, which is a powerful part of walking in the freedom Jesus wants for us."

--*Karen Rissinger, MA, School Psychologist and wife of the author.*

"I could have used this bit of advice for the past 50 years! Pastor Joel's attempt at making us understand what forgiveness is and what it's not had me questioning why my mind and soul have been so troubled over things God had already taken care of. I now know what a great tribute it is to God when I can honestly say, 'I forgive, let's get on with it!' Pastor Joel is a preacher who without preaching, gives a thought-provoking sermon on forgiveness in terms that are often riveting & amusing."

--*David Tedeschi, President, Newington Chapter, Rotary International*

To my wife of 34 years, Karen. Thank you for your love and forgiveness toward me and for the example you set daily. Love you more and more every day!

To my granddaughters Aadi and Bryn. I pray that you'll both grow-up living in the freedom of forgiveness. First, the forgiveness that comes from a faith commitment to Jesus. But also in the blessing of sharing that forgiveness with those who may hurt you. I love you both—Your Bompa…

To our wonderful LifeWay Office Manager Charity Lane. Thank you for a million things you do every week to keep us moving forward, but a special thanks for your help with this book.

To our Artistic Designer/Genius Linda Porter—you made this book and so many other projects SHINE! Thank you so much!

To Pastor Steve and the staff and members at LifeWay. Thank you for the blessing of serving with you in reaching "the one."

FORWARD

When it comes to relationships, nothing is more important than forgiveness. I've watched the lack of it destroy marriages, friendships, businesses and churches for much of my adult life and career. It often seems to be the single most difficult thing to process. As a culture, the list of things we find "unforgiveable" seems to grow at an exponential rate.

And yet, at its core, forgiveness is so simple, so profound, and so powerful—it literally has the power to change everything in an instant.

So why don't we give it or seek it?

I'm convinced that we have allowed forgiveness to become FAR more complicated than it truly needs to be. We think it is difficult and confusing. We stumble over various "necessities" which have become attached to the act of forgiving and yet, frankly, are false. The attachments or supposed "necessities" often have little or nothing to do with true forgiveness.

And, according to Jesus, it's critical that we get this right! When sharing the parable of the unjust creditor, he said, "*And his master was angry, and delivered him to the torturers until he should pay all that was due to him. So My heavenly Father also will do to you if each of you, from his heart, does not forgive his brother his trespasses* (Matt. 18:34-35)."

Ouch! In the Lord's Prayer we frequently recite, "Forgive us our debts as we forgive our debtors," showing a connection between our being forgiven and our willingness to GRANT forgiveness. Yet, it seems so hard, so complicated, and frankly so impossible.

I've watched people struggle with this issue when applied to some of the most egregious sins imaginable. Without clarity and simplification, they are trapped. Even their personal relationship with God is in jeopardy.

Thus this book...

My desire is to create a simple, faith-based, clear manual which will:

1. Strip-away the fallacies by discussing what forgiveness is not…

2. And simply explain what forgiveness is.

The desired outcome is that the reader will be free— free to forgive and thus realize an even GREATER freedom from bitterness, anger, hurt, resentment, depression, and more.

To that end,

Pastor Joel

The Forgiveness Fallacies

Part I: What Forgiveness Isn't….

CHAPTER ONE: FORGIVENESS IS <u>NOT</u> RECONCILIATION

"Obviously, you haven't forgiven me! If you had, you would _____ (fill in the blank) with me." The blank could contain any number of options: "Live," "Sleep," "be friends," "hang-out," you name it—the point is, when someone says this, they are tying forgiveness to reconciliation.

But it isn't—in fact, it literally CAN'T be.

How would you forgive a dead person if reconciliation was a necessity? Scary thought huh? In fact, if there's a supernatural enemy of mankind who WANTS people trapped in unforgiveness (and I believe there is), this is a perfect method for Him. If you convince people that you have to reconcile in order to forgive, dead offenders make this an inescapable trap!

Now don't misunderstand, forgiveness is necessary for reconciliation to occur. If you hurt me and I never forgive you, the chances of us restoring our relationship are a big fat ZERO. Still, forgiveness and reconciliation are NOT the same thing and frankly, sometimes it's downright dangerous to reconcile with someone even AFTER you've forgiven them.

I've watched this as a pastor for over 25 years, especially with abusive husbands. The classic scenario is that he beats his wife, she finally runs away (usually after multiple pleading appeals from someone like me counseling her), and he comes to her on bended knee—telling her he's sorry and asking for forgiveness. She, and sadly many people in her life, believes that if she TRULY forgives him, she'll move back in with him. Wanting to be a good Christian wife, she does…

And the beating goes on. Sometimes resulting in her death.

So sad…and so unnecessary.

The simple truth is that reconciliation has other pieces to it. Primarily, it requires repentance on the part of the perpetrator. In other words, it's not enough for him to say, "I'm sorry, please forgive me, it will never happen again." True reconciliation requires change and evidence or fruit of change.

John the Baptist understood this well. Faced with a sudden onslaught of Pharisees wanting to be baptized to demonstrate their piety to the crowds, John said, *"Brood of vipers! Who warned you to flee from the wrath to come? Therefore bear fruits worthy of repentance, and do not begin to say to yourselves, 'We have Abraham as our father.' For I say to you that God is able to raise up children to Abraham from these stones. And even now the ax is laid to the root of the trees. Therefore every tree which does not bear good fruit is cut down and thrown into the fire." So the people asked him, saying, "What shall we do then?" He answered and said to them, "He who has two tunics, let him give to him who has none; and he who has food, let him do likewise." Then tax collectors also came to be baptized, and said to him, "Teacher, what shall we do?" And he said to them, "Collect no more than what is appointed for you." Likewise the soldiers asked him, saying, "And what shall we do?" So he said to them, "Do not intimidate anyone or accuse falsely, and be content with your wages.* (Luke 3:7-14)"

John is telling them, "Look—saying you believe and going through the ceremonial motions isn't enough. I want to see evidence that you're REALLY changing and at least trying to follow Jesus before I'll dunk you!"

And rightly so....

Repentance means a change of direction. In the Greek of the New Testament, the word most often translated "repent" literally means, "to turn." Thus, a repentant person changes—turns around and moves away from what he/she was doing. I would argue that true reconciliation and a bond of friendship CANNOT occur after serious hurt UNLESS repentance occurs first.

Say for example I had an anger problem expressed by stomping on peoples' toes and breaking them. Furthermore, let's say I had broken three of your toes on separate occasions but asked you to "forgive" me and thus hang-out with me again and again. After 2-3 offenses, it would be wiser, and I would argue more Christian, to not only refuse to hang-out with me, but to force me to get counseling and help, file a restraining order on me, and perhaps invest in some steel-toed boots just in case you ran into me at the mall.

Why? And why would I suggest that this is a "more Christian" response?

Let's ponder this. If you keep "forgiving" by also reconciling with me, you've made several damaging mistakes:

1. You've put yourself at repeated risk. You might think this is Christian in that you're "turning the other cheek," or forgiving "77 times." In truth this

would be a misinterpretation of Scripture, still—practically speaking—you're going to lose more toes.

2. You've taught me a lie and thus done me harm as well. You've told me by your actions that all I need to do is say I'm sorry and things will "go back to normal." You'll spend time with me as if nothing happened if I only mouth the words, "I'm sorry," and/or "I won't do it again." You've told me that repentance isn't important—just good intentions or, perhaps just "good words." This will create more harm for me in the long-run as I continue to live this out in other aspects of my life.

3. You've put others at risk of harm as well. You see, if I truly believe that no change is necessary, only nice words; then it's VERY likely I'll continue this behavior with other friends, family, coworkers, etc. Soon, there will be an entire army of broken-toed people wandering the neighborhood because I've learned that it's OK to break toes as long as you say you're sorry and ask for forgiveness.

CRAZINESS!

We'll cover the simple truth of what forgiveness really is and how to grant it later in this book. For now, let's consider how separating it from reconciliation might work in the "toe-breaking" scenario above.

First, while you might let me do it twice, thinking that the first time was truly an accident, a healthy biblical and relational approach would be to file charges with the police and tell me to get help, seek counseling, and stay away until things have changed. Next, you'd likely want to get some protection like the steel-toed boots I mentioned and, if I'm exceptionally hostile, a restraining order too. You'd resolve to stay away and make sure I stayed away until I demonstrated true change/repentance.

Next, you'd forgive me. Now this is something that happens between you and God. We'll look at it in depth later, but the point is that you've really chosen to forgive and given me—and what I did—to Him and trusted Him to handle it. You'd then ask Him to heal your damaged emotions.

After time passed, you might be able to reconcile IF I had done the following:

1. Expressed true remorse.

2. Sought help and/or counsel for change.

3. Shown evidence of that change in my life.

Assuming these things were in place, you could slowly work back toward reconciliation. You might first spend time with me in a larger group (while still wearing those shoes we talked about). Next, you'd spend time with me in a smaller group—still having others there as a witness and to help should I "lose it." If all goes well…you might experiment with a few one-on-one meetings in a very public place.

If I truly have changed, and you've truly forgiven me, reconciliation may be possible. Still, you would have to understand that these are separate, independent components or steps in the process. Mixing them or somehow ignoring repentance as part of the process is a dangerous and damaging mistake.

On the other hand, when we properly understand and separate forgiveness from reconciliation, we're one step closer to freedom—the freedom that comes from being able to truly and completely forgive anyone of virtually anything such that anger, bitterness, hurt, discouragement, depression and other symptoms literally disappear....

Ah, but reconciliation is not the only forgiveness fallacy. Let's look at another in chapter two....

Chapter Two: Forgiveness is NOT Justification

While unspoken, this is perhaps the most common assumptions about forgiveness. We believe that in order to forgive, we must be able to justify the behavior of the perpetrator. We might look to their past or some injustice done to them which, apparently, makes the harm they inflicted on us—"understandable."

We say things like, "Well, I know he screamed, cursed at me, and threw rocks at my head; but I understand. I had insulted him and I know that his father used to throw rocks at him when he was little, so that's all he knows. That's his learned response."

Let's translate that—"So…due to the fact that he was abused as a child and the fact that you said some things to him that were harsh, his attempt to crush your skull with a bolder is permissible and thus forgivable.

Really?

I once counseled a woman whose earliest memory was being tortured and sexually molested by several men wearing black hoods. It was part of a satanic ritual performed by a cult which her father led. Thus, one of the men abusing her was her father. Can you imagine ANY explanation whereby his behavior was "understandable" or in some way, "justified?"

Never!

So there's the trap. If you can't justify or understand it, you can't forgive it. Now we're back to the same place. God is demanding that we forgive, but in this case, it's impossible. This paints an ugly picture of God. He requires us to do the impossible in order to connect with Him. Thankfully, that's NOT the God we worship!

Let's "get real" for a moment. There are some sins, some infractions, some violent or sadistic acts that just can't be rationalized or justified. They are just evil. Period! True forgiveness doesn't require our rational explanation of cause and effect. Thus, when we understand it, we don't have to somehow explain away this kind of evil.

Frankly, what does it say about us as a society when we even TRY to justify evil. As I write this, we've seen yet another mass shooting of innocent people in Toronto, ON. Listening to talk radio, I'm amazed at how authorities, news anchors, and commentators will search for a cause. Many are afraid to consider religious motives, normally Islamic terrorism, even if evidence supports that. Still, they'll look for mental illness, a history of violent abuse or neglect, a recent break-up, drug abuse or virtually ANYTHING to explain and somehow "make sense" of what is at its core—NOT SENSIBLE! In truth, it's just evil. And, as we'll see later, we need no more explanation than that to truly forgive.

The old adage, "two wrongs don't make a right" comes to mind here as well. Even IF we can explain why the person acted the way they did, treating others poorly is never justified by our own past hurts. Apart from the issue of forgiveness, what happens when we think we CAN find a justification for harm? In those cases aren't we just enabling more bad behavior? Don't we, by virtue of our rational explanation, make it possible for the perpetrator and others—to do the same thing again, and again…and again?!

Of course we do.

I've watched this over the years when dealing with addictive behavior and co-dependency. Once, a woman in our church asked me to visit her and her alcoholic husband. "He needs and wants help," she told me. "Of course," I replied, "I'd be glad to help if I can."

Within 5 minutes of my arrival at their home, it became obvious to me that she had lied. When I brought-up his drinking, the husband said, "I don't care." "But you are in danger of losing your job," I said. "I don't care," was his response. I brought-up the potential loss of his marriage, his family relationships, his money, his home, and most of all—his relationship with Christ and His Church. "I don't care," he honestly told me, "I just love to drink."

The amazing thing about this conversation was what happened in the middle of it. During a stream of consciousness, he interrupted himself to ask his wife for some money. He didn't attempt to hide the fact that he was going to the package store to buy booze. Without missing a beat, she reached into her purse and pulled out a $20 bill.

I had heard and seen enough. While making it clear to the man that he was choosing to worship booze and not God, thus guaranteeing a tormented future both in this life and the next, I thanked him for his honesty in not wasting my time by pretending to go through counseling or a recovery program, etc., with no real intent to change.

I then turned to her and "let her have it" as well. I told her that by making excuses for him, misrepresenting his intentions, and giving him money to continue his sinful/destructive habit, she was just as guilty.

Justifying evil is embracing evil. Thank God, this has no part in the act of forgiving ourselves or others.

And, in our next chapter, we'll take a closer look at ourselves and the need to empathize in order to be motivated to forgive....

Chapter Three: Forgiveness is NOT Empathy

Another common fallacy is that we must be able to identify with those who hurt us in order to forgive them. Or, put another way, if I can feel for and relate to the one who does me harm, I'll be able to more easily forgive.

Now I realize that empathy CAN help soften our hearts in preparation for forgiveness. I may find it easier to be in a spirit of forgiveness if I can empathize with the person who hurt me. As Paul says to the Ephesians, "…be kind to one another and tenderhearted, forgiving one another, even as God in Christ forgave you (Eph 4:32)." Also, empathy can help us AFTER we've forgiven as we ask God to heal our damaged emotions over time (See Part II of this book for more on this subject).

But, there are a couple of pitfalls here. First, if I think that empathy is the same as forgiveness or that it's a prerequisite, I might be trapped. If the evil done to me was so illogical, vile, and incomprehensible; I may not be able to empathize and thus…I'm trapped in unforgiveness again.

Next, there's the problem of what I'll call "over-empathy." This is dangerous. Why? Well, for starters, if I get really good at empathizing with people who do damage to me and others, isn't it more likely that I'll begin to ACT more like those people? In other words, I'll begin hurting others too and excusing my behavior as I go.

This is the Jeremiah 17:9 core of our fallen nature. Our natural hearts are deceitful in that we always feel our motives are pure—no matter what we do. So, we have a need to excuse bad behavior in ourselves. Thus, when we're hurt, we're afraid to become too critical of the perpetrator because we think, "Who am I to judge?" We feel that if we can empathize with what, and why harm was done, it will be easier to accept our own failings. And, in the process, we've now begun to justify sinful behavior.

This is because of our human nature. Post Genesis chapter three, we are all narcissists. The world revolves around us.

We think we are the arbiters of justice, mercy, fairness, truth, good and evil. This is the result of our ancestors, Adam and Eve, eating from the tree of the knowledge of good and evil. We all now act as if WE are gods.

So…follow me here…if I can empathize and connect someone to me by relating to and "understanding" what they did, I can forgive them because if they are in some way like me, they must be good.

Biblical, true forgiveness is NEVER based on my own righteousness. I don't forgive people because of my goodness, rather, I forgive them despite my own sinful nature and weakness. We'll look at this later.

And, as with other fallacies, there's a trap here also. What if the crime against me is so ugly, so heinous, so violent and evil that I literally can't find a way to empathize? What if I'm so hurt, I can't relate? Again, I'm stuck! I'm stuck in unforgiveness and all the bitterness, anger, and ugliness that goes with it.

So…if we CAN empathize with the offender, we are vulnerable to becoming like him/her. In that case we can't really forgive since all we're doing is accepting the offender due to our love of self. And, if we can't relate to/empathize with them, we're still stuck in the trap of bitterness and unforgiveness.

It's a true catch-22. And yet, it's so common. I hear it often. For example, a husband will cheat on his wife. She, when hearing about it, says, "Well, I almost cheated on him a couple of years ago and I like reading Harlequin Romance novels, so I understand." In other words, she in essence says, "I'm sinful too, so I can look the other way and 'forgive' because he's human like me."

True forgiveness, again, has nothing to do with my ability to relate to evil behavior. It has nothing to do with my understanding of bad people or their behavior. It's not based on my goodness or my sinfulness…it's based on something MUCH greater.

More on that later, but first let's look at another common fallacy—the fallacy of forgetfulness....

Chapter Four: Forgiveness Is Not Forgetting

For Christians, this fallacy begins with a false idea about God. It goes something like this: "Well, we know God forgets because the Bible says He removes our sins and remembers them no more (Jeremiah 31:34 and Psalm 103:12)."

Most Christians believe this. So, the argument is that if God forgets when He forgives, so must/should we! The result is both divisive and guilt-producing. If we have a negative memory of a past offense, we feel guilty for that thought. Worse yet, if we mention any element of a past offence to someone who has hurt us, they will likely accuse us of not forgiving them. Hurts, arguments, and worse can result.

Forgiveness and forgetfulness are NOT the same thing. Furthermore, God doesn't literally forget all of our past sins or He'd be an Alzheimer's patient. In fact, half of the Bible would suddenly go blank since David's sin with Bathsheba,

Peter's denial of Jesus, Abraham's lies about Sarah, and much more would vanish. We'd have blank pages or perhaps redacted sections "blacked-out" as with top secret CIA documents.

I would argue that rather than forget our sins, God has owned them. Isn't that what the cross is all about? Jesus took our sin upon himself. He not only knows what they are, He has the stripes and scars to prove that He took responsibility for them. The penalty is paid, but, thankfully, He didn't forget! No, He forgave!

Even verses that seem to indicate God's forgetfulness re. our past often have different meaning in the original Hebrew. When studied, these texts speak of God not "recalling our sins to our account." In other words, He has taken them off our ledger and put them on HIS own.

I think of this like a bank statement. Let's say I had an overdraft charge on my checking account, but due to hardship, I contest it. The bank may choose to remove it, but does this mean it is literally "forgotten?" No. It simply means it was transferred from my ledger or statement to the banks.'

As to our human responsibility, forgetting is frankly impossible. We literally remember everything that has ever happened to us. Psychologists tell us that it's all stored in our brains. We may or may not be able to recall all of it, but it's there. Sometimes, the recall is involuntary. We hear a song or see a color or a picture that triggers a memory and WHAM—there it is! Is this a sign of a lack of forgiveness?

No! It's simply a normal physiological response. Thus, it's quite unfair to hold a memory of past hurts against ourselves or others. It's not reasonable for someone else to expect us to literally be unable to recall what they did.

Having said that, we DO have a responsibility to deal wisely and lovingly with those memories. We must forgive and, while we can't forget, we shouldn't use those memories as weapons to "beat people over the head" to cause guilt and shame.

I have found that when I truly forgive, the memories of past infractions aren't as painful as they were. Oh, they're not pleasant memories to be sure. Still, they don't carry the emotional weight and impact they once did.

And, speaking of feelings, in our next chapter we'll look at the fallacy of emotions and forgiveness. Is it true that you must "feel like forgiving," to TRULY forgive?

Chapter Five: Forgiveness is NOT a Feeling!

Perhaps the most common fallacy regarding forgiveness is that you must "feel like forgiving" in order to "truly forgive." This actually reflects a larger problem in our culture—the idea that feelings determine truth.

Not to turn this chapter into a philosophy lesson, but postmodernity and the concept of relative versus absolute truth form the foundation of this concept. Postmodern thinking became increasingly popular during the 20th Century. The basic tenant is that absolute truth doesn't exist. All truth and assumptions are based on personal preference making "truth" relative. Even religious leaders have "bought into" this lie. College professors and other leaders have popularized sayings like, "What's true for me is true for me and what's true for you is true for you."

Of course, this is nonsense. Science has proven that there are God-given laws in our universe. Gravity for instance is an absolute reality. I can deny it all I want. I can ignore it whenever possible. Still, if you believe in gravity and I do not, we'll both splatter and die should we leap from the top of the Empire State Building without a parachute. Our opinion of "truth" regarding gravity will not affect the reality of its existence.

As an aside, I would add that this worldview has impacted how many Christians see faith. To many, faith is a feeling. Thus they think that if you have a strong enough faith/feeling about something, God will do it or grant it for you. Romans 10:17 tells us that real faith is based solely on what God says. What I feel or think or want is irrelevant regarding true biblical faith. Thus faith is not relative in a postmodern sense. It's based on truth. And, what Jesus says is true because He IS the truth (John 14:6). I can either choose to believe it or not—regardless of how I feel about it.

So back to our postmodern view of feelings and forgiveness. The "logic" flows something like this: since there is no absolute truth, then all "truth" is subjective and relative. And, since truth is subjective, what you "feel" is true is "true for you." Conversely, what you don't feel is false for you. Therefore, to say you forgive someone when you don't feel like it is—a lie.

Yet another trap.

Let's go back to the story I told you about the woman with early memories of satanic torture. If she had told me that she woke up that morning "feeling like forgiving" those men, I would have questioned her sanity. In fact, I'd wonder about her sense of justice, morality, virtue, etc. It would be inappropriate and rationally impossible for her to feel like forgiving men who would sexually torture a 3 year old!

Yet, God commands that we forgive. So, (and here's the satanic strategy to this), God asks us to do something that's impossible since we can't "feel like it," yet we must "feel like it," to make it true. So…God is unfair, unreasonable, and cruel.

What a load of nonsense!

The truth is…truth is absolute because at its core, truth is who and what God is. Truth is what He says. And, since He doesn't change, His Word is reliable and rock solid. Thus we have to believe that if He commands us to forgive, it can't be based on feelings which come and go, ebb and flow, uncontrollably.

I think of our psyche like a train. The engine is our mind, the cars in the middle represent our actions based on will, and the caboose—that's our emotions or feelings. The problem is that most people try to let the caboose lead the train. There are several problems with this. First, you can't steer the caboose. Second, the caboose has no power of itself since the combustion engine isn't there. Finally, the caboose is in the back of the train. Thus, if it "leads," we're going backwards.

Think about that for a minute….

Even when the train is connected properly and moving forward, the caboose might be a long way behind the engine if there are a lot of cars in the middle. If the train goes around a corner, the caboose might even be out of sight and seemingly going in a different direction. Still, since it's attached, it will eventually come into view and in line with the engine. To "trust" it to navigate and drive would however, be a disaster.

In the days of the old steam rails, the caboose was for pleasure. It was the place for the crew to relax, have a glass of brandy and enjoy the view. It was a place of respite and escape during a long journey. That's a blessing. But to let the caboose lead? That would be a curse.

Yet, I have counseled and coached hundreds who let their caboose/emotions lead them. God never meant it to be that way. This is especially true when we speak of forgiveness. When practically understood, forgiveness is an act of will coming into line with God's truth. Feelings may lag behind—even miles behind and around the bend. Still, they eventually line up if the train remains intact/attached. Thus, once you choose to forgive, you'll eventually find your damaged emotions heal and settle.

But note that the strategy of the Enemy creates a "catch-22" for forgiveness. If you think you must "feel like" forgiving, but you don't/can't feel better and see your emotions stabilize until you forgive—you're stuck, stuck, STUCK! Rather, choose to forgive as we'll cover later, and watch your feelings come into line.

Chapter Six: Forgiveness Isn't Amnesty!

From time-to-time, we hear of a government leader granting amnesty to a criminal. Sometimes, the motives for these moves are questionable. Still, the concept is that they basically ignore and completely remove the crime and conviction from the perpetrator's record. He/she is free of penalty. It's as if the infraction never happened.

We've already covered the fallacy of forgetting when we forgive. Still, we need to think through the ramifications of a thinking that true forgiveness is like amnesty. It is not. In fact, applying amnesty to forgiveness might be the worst thing we could do for the perpetrator and the victim.

For example, I've had to deal with the presence of pedophiles in our community. Science has proven that once someone "crosses the bridge" of acting on a sexual urge toward children, it is virtually impossible for them to return to a normal adult sex life and avoid doing it again. Thus, they must be banned from working with children. They must be watched when at a family gathering where children are present. They cannot be treated as if the sin never occurred. This is for the benefit of the children they might abuse, but it's also for their own benefit to avoid being arrested, or worse.

In these cases, granting amnesty would be a mistake. Yet, we're still commanded to forgive. Letting someone suffer the penalty for their poor choices doesn't negate forgiveness. Forgiveness is a separate act altogether.

I remember when our son was about 2-3 years old. He was obsessed with the stove. We had to watch him constantly because he wanted to touch the burners. We would sternly tell him, "No!" That didn't work. We would slap his hand and restate the "No!" That didn't work either. He was determined to touch the hot burner.

So…one day when he had been particularly persistent, I decided to let him touch it. I told him "No," he went for it anyway and I just stood fast. Sure enough, he touched it, I put ice on the burn, it healed quickly, and his burner-grabbing days came to an end. He never tried to touch the stove again.

This idea often becomes a challenge for victims of crime. They think that they must refuse to press charges if they've forgiven someone. I totally disagree. True love for victim and abuser alike often means letting the justice system do its thing such that penalties are experienced and lessons are (hopefully) learned. Forgiveness can and often should be practiced without amnesty.

Having said all this, we should then consider what a lack of forgiveness actually does, or doesn't do, to the guilty party. Legal penalties aside, does it REALLY hurt someone to refuse to forgive them?

That depends.

If they're dead, the answer is obviously, "No." If they're alive, it will only hurt them if they desire a relationship with us and we're refusing that based on our bitterness, etc. In my experience, most perpetrators are either ignorant of the harm they've done or frankly, just don't care. Thus, our lack of forgiveness is irrelevant to them.

So...who does our lack of forgiveness hurt? Normally, only us. Thus, while forgiveness isn't amnesty in the truest sense/meaning of that word, in essence, WE get amnesty when we forgive...even though they may not. And while our emotional healing may take time, our act of forgiving and thus setting ourselves free, can happen in an instant....

More on that in our next chapter....

Chapter Seven: Forgiveness Is NOT a Process!

I wish I had the proverbial dollar for every time I've heard of a counselor or pastor telling someone that forgiveness will "take time," or that "it's a process." This is great for generating more revenue if you're being paid by the hour to counsel people through a crisis. Still, when evaluated through the lens of scripture and practical experience…

It's phony-baloney!

I would argue that this idea is based on the falsehood we covered earlier re. feelings. Feelings DO take time to heal. But, as we've already proven, forgiveness is not a feeling.

Still, some folks smarter than I would suggest that there are stages to forgiveness. Thus, it happens over time—perhaps a long time. Once we've delved into a truly biblical description of forgiveness this will become clearer. Still, suffice it to say for now that forgiveness literally comes as a result of a choice made in a moment of time. There may be stages of understanding and clarity that come first. Still, forgiveness itself does not take a long period of time.

Believing that it does take time or is a process presents yet another trap by the Devil. If I am repeatedly told that it won't happen right away, it allows me to justify putting it off. All I need to say is, "I'm not ready yet" and everyone will back off and leave me in my misery of bitterness, hurt, pain, loss, etc.

Over the years I've watched people who told me they "couldn't forgive" certain other people, do just that during a one-day prayer process called, "Steps to Freedom in Christ." This process was created and popularized by Dr. Neil T. Anderson. You can find out more at our website, www.ctcfministry.com. Frankly half the battle is convincing them that this WON'T take time and is a decision made in a moment. Once they see it, they're normally able to tearfully and powerfully forgive and move on with their lives.

So…how do we do this? What IS forgiveness and how do we grant it. Furthermore, how can it set us free to experience many other blessings in life? These and other similar questions will be answered in the second half of this book. We'll start with the basics—how forgiveness, at its core, is a simple choice!

Part II: What Forgiveness Truly Is….

Chapter Eight: Forgiveness Is…A Choice!

At the end of the day, forgiveness is quite simple. It's a choice. It's a choice to be for, giving to God.

But giving what?

Better asked, "Giving whom?" In essence, when you forgive someone, you're formally giving that person, what they did, and how it made you feel to God. After all, He alone is the perfect judge. If they need discipline or punishment, He's more than capable. On the other hand, if they repent or if your perception of what they did is off, He's also more than capable of extending mercy.

That brings up a good point. Part of this whole process is realizing that sometimes our perception of what was done or why it was done can be wrong. I remember a woman approaching me during a communion service at a church I pastored. As she and others were coming forward, she leaned over to me and said, "Pastor, I forgive you." That's great…but to this day, I couldn't tell you a single thing that I did to offend or hurt her. Honestly, I always thought we had a great friendship and I'm clueless as to why she would need to forgive me. In her case, I would certainly hope that God would extend grace to this poor pastor-perpetrator who has no idea what he did wrong!

In fact, it's entirely possible that I did nothing wrong. Over the years, I've watched people get offended and break relationship with others over misunderstandings, imputed motives, false rumors, lies from the Enemy, gossip, and more. They need to forgive those who they feel hurt them to be sure. Still, God will not hold supposed infractions against the innocent. Yet another reason that He alone is the perfect judge and the one who to whom we need to be "for, giving" our offenses.

This means I can also forgive God. Now I know how that sounds, but let's consider this. While we know God doesn't sin or do anything wrong, we also know that there are times when we are hurt or angry based on our understanding of what we feel He should have done differently on our behalf. We may wonder why He didn't stop us from being abused by someone else. We may wonder why He didn't heal someone we love. Whatever the cause, we're hurt and angry. We need to be for, giving that hurt to Him and trusting that He has it all under control and that his loving, merciful, just nature will someday make this all clear. We're literally "letting go and letting God" take away the pain, bitterness, anger, confusion, etc....

When we forgive, we simply choose and state out loud that we choose to forgive the person for what they did/didn't do. We state how it made us feel. Then we ask God to heal our damaged emotions.

In a nutshell, that's it!

This understanding also allows us to forgive ourselves. I can choose to give myself and my sins to God, just as I can do so for others. When I do this, I'm simply acknowledging the reality that He is in charge and that I don't have control. I'm letting the shed blood of Christ apply to what I've done and I'm refusing to hold my sin "over my own head."

I've often talked to people who refuse to forgive themselves for some serious mistake in the past. Usually, they are afraid to let it go and give it to God because they think this will minimize it and make it easier to repeat the offense/sin. In reality, this is an insult to Christ.

I know that sounds harsh. Still, think about it. If I think that refusing to forgive myself will result in more positive change than letting Jesus take it and giving the Holy Spirit power to transform me, I'm saying that God is not great enough to help me grow.

Wow!

It's as if I'm standing next to the cross watching Jesus bleed and gasp for breath. Then, instead of trusting that sacrifice and all it avails, I say, "Nice try Lord, but I've got a better way. I'm going to refuse to forgive myself and let guilt and shame motivate me for the rest of my life." None of us would say that at that moment, yet, when we refuse to forgive ourselves, that's EXACTLY what we're doing.

And, when we make that decision regarding ourselves or others, we're choosing to stay in bondage. We will remain in the bondage of bitterness, fear, shame, anger, and virtually every negative emotion imaginable. The chain we attach to others and/or to ourselves is always attached to us. Thus, we end-up suffering. We are hindered and trapped.

Satan and those who serve Him also latch on to these chains. They will torment and attack at will because our disobedience via a lack of forgiveness opens the door for them to destroy, distract, discourage, etc.

In my experience, a lack of forgiveness leads to many other problems and, in fact, is the root cause of many sins, illnesses, and relationship problems. I've seen it lead to a lack of faith. I've watched it destroy marriages. Furthermore, I've seen it result in excessive lust, addiction to porn, alcoholism, drug abuse, and more.

This is because frankly, refusing to forgive ourselves and others is a sin. It's an act of direct disobedience to the command of Christ as explained earlier.

Knowing that forgiveness is a choice to give God control of the offense, the offender, all of it—is so freeing. Knowing that it isn't a process, a matter of forgetting or reconciling, etc.; makes it much easier.

Now let's talk about the actual moment of forgiveness…what does that entail?

Chapter Nine: Forgiveness IS a Moment

This chapter probably belongs as an appendix to chapter seven, "Forgiveness Is NOT a Process." Still, understanding the moment when forgiveness takes place is critical.

I should probably clarify that I understand the steps leading up to the moment of forgiveness. I realize that we often need to process some anger and achieve clarity on what happened to us and how it has hurt us. For severe losses or trauma, we need to cycle through the shock, denial, anger, and grief that normally follows.

Still, as soon as we know what happened, who is responsible for it, and how it has made us feel; it's time to choose to forgive. Waiting beyond that will only hurt us more.

I also recognize that the healing which inevitably follows forgiveness takes place over time and is in that sense a process. Emotions, the caboose, take a while to come into line with the rest of the train. Still, this can't happen until we reach the moment of forgiveness and choose to process it as an act of free will.

The problem is that we often reach the moment of forgiveness and understand the choice, but we refuse to make it. We put it off or somehow mystically think that it will "just happen naturally." Let me assure you—this is never going to happen. Apart from an intentional decision, you will not forgive and thus, you'll remain trapped in your own personal hell-on-earth.

My advice is to "seize the moment." Perhaps that moment is right now. You know of someone, or several someone's who need forgiveness. You've understood what it isn't and you recognize it's a choice of giving them and what they did to God's sovereign control.

If this describes you, why not make a list. Ask God to show you if there are others you need to forgive as well. Write down all of the names of people who come to mind. Once you've got what you feel is a complete list, simply pray the following prayer:

> *"Lord, I choose to forgive _____ (name of the person) for _____ (what they did or didn't do), because it made me feel _____. I choose not to seek retribution or vengeance. I ask you to bless them and now heal my damaged emotions. In Jesus' name, Amen!"*

The result is…well, it's a miracle. More on that in chapter ten.

Chapter Ten: Forgiveness IS a Miracle

It's good for us at this point to have what I'll call a "spiritual reality-check." We've already seen that when we withhold forgiveness, it really doesn't hurt anyone but us. But there's a Theological/Biblical foundation for that.

In brief, who are WE to deny forgiveness? If Jesus was tortured and murdered—paying the penalty for our sins— how DARE we deny someone else the same?

This has ramifications not only regarding our ability to forgive others, it has impact on our willingness to lead others to Christ as well. Jesus made clear the connection when he told his disciples that they had the power to grant forgiveness or the lack thereof regarding their mission (see John 20:23 and Acts 8:22). When we share the gospel, we make it possible for others to be forgiven. When we don't…well…we don't!

This is painful, but it needs to be addressed. We literally have no right to withhold forgiveness or the possibility of it from anyone! Where we have, we need to repent!!

Think about this. Even if we detach all of the false baggage normally associated with forgiveness and summarize it as a choice to give to God our hurts and those who hurt us, who do we really think we are when we refuse? Are we better than God? Are we more "just?" Do we have the right to punish others? Do we have the right to punish ourselves?

And, if we understand the miracle of grace, how DARE we deny it to others by not forgiving them (as if that were even a possible result)? How dare we withhold it by not sharing our faith with them or participating in the Great Commission of Matthew 28:19-20?!!

Imagine yourself standing at the foot of the cross watching Jesus die. As He's gasping for breath and bleeding from multiple open wounds, imagine yourself arguing with Him.

Would you say, "*Well done Lord! I really appreciate you doing this for me. My sins are many and your stripes are much appreciated. Still, I just wanted to let you know that I can't extend forgiveness to _____ (fill in the blank) because their sin was worse than mine. And, while I know you're forgiving them just like those you just asked the Father to forgive a minute ago, I just can't—or, honestly, I just won't! Also, regarding my non-Christian friends, I'm not going to share you with them either. It's just too hard, too embarrassing, and frankly—just too time consuming. So, thanks again, but just don't expect me to extend this courtesy of yours to anyone else OK?*"

Absurd!

And yet, isn't this EXACTLY what we're doing when we refuse forgiveness to others or refuse to obey Christ's command to be His witnesses (see Acts 1:8)? We're telling Him that His sacrifice is just for us, not for those who hurt or offend us. We're telling Him that grace and salvation is ours, but we wish to deny it to those around us.

Again, who the heck do we think we are?!!

How dare we withhold the miracle of forgiveness from others? The God and Creator of the universe chose from the foundation of the world to take on our penalty so that we could spend eternity with Him. He put off the trappings of divinity, humbled himself by entering the womb of an unmarried, poor, teenage girl in a tiny little village in the middle of nowhere. He lived a sinless, yet largely lackluster life until age 30 when he spent a brief stint preaching, healing, helping, feeding, and teaching a relative handful of people who largely rejected, denied, tortured, and crucified Him.

Why?

So those who would choose to, could have forgiveness. They could let HIM take their lies, their lusts, their hatred and more so they could appear before a sinless, flawless God and be seen the same way. NO other world religion has a god who would die for His people. All others demand excessive obedience to works/rituals, self-denial, extravagant sacrifice and STILL make no guarantees re. the future spiritual state of their devotees.

It's a mystery, it's mind-blowing. It truly is a miracle!

So, it should be our joy to not only receive this blessing, but to share it. In a small way, we share it by extending forgiveness when we're hurt. In a much larger way, we share it when we tell people about Jesus and how forgiveness and eternal life can be theirs by faith.

Jesus paid a heavy penalty to make this possible. We honor that when we offer it. But, while Jesus paid the ultimate penalty, personal forgiveness is not without a personal cost. Let's look at that in Chapter Eleven.

Chapter Eleven: Forgiveness IS a Sacrifice

Let's say you didn't like the last chapter and, in your rage, you chased me down and chopped-off my right arm. Ouch!

Thanks a lot!

Now, if I'm going to practice what I preach, I need to forgive you. I'll need to choose to give you and what you did to God, acknowledging that it made me feel crippled, emotionally wounded, and limited in my ability to do some of the things I love to do.

Then what?

Well, at the end of the prayer, I'd ask God to heal my damaged emotions and, over time, He would. Right? Of course!

But I'd still be missing an arm.

Now please don't send me email about how God can regrow limbs. I know He can. My point is, he rarely does! Normally, if you cut off my arm, it would NOT grow back and, even after forgiveness and emotional healing, I'd still be a one-armed author.

And that's part of the cost of forgiveness. Part of this process is being willing to live with the consequences of other people's actions. This sounds difficult—and it can be—but it's not unusual. In fact, I would argue that we all do this daily, whether we've forgiven others or not.

Adam and Eve made a foul choice in the Garden (Genesis 3). Like it or not, we all live with the consequences of that choice for our entire lives! Our parents made choices about life which have impacted us—sometimes negatively—and we live with those. Going back to my dismembering example above, whether or not I chose to forgive you, I'd still be living without an arm.

The truth is, as Dr. Neil Anderson has written, we all live with the consequences of other people's sins.[1] Our choice is to either do so in peace or with bitterness, hurt, anger, demonic strongholds, and a whole host of other problems!!

I choose the former, not the latter option!

Still, it's important for us to accept the reality. Denying it can lead to a backlash of disappointment. It's part of counting the cost. Forgiveness comes with a price. True, Jesus paid the primary price. Still, we have a piece of this in terms of the natural consequences of living in a fallen world. We'd be remiss if we didn't accept that. We must do so…and, we'll discuss more of the necessity of forgiveness in our next chapter.

Chapter Twelve: Forgiveness IS a Necessity

Knowing that I'm a pastor, you probably expect me to say that forgiveness is a necessity because God commands it. And, while that would be true, I always try to look deeper and consider why God commands whatever He commands.

Since God is love, whatever he commands is for our good. We've already seen that a lack of forgiveness leaves us trapped in bitterness, anger, and emotional pain which can even lead to physical health problems. We've explored the connection between our relationship to God and our willingness to forgive others.

But wait—there's more!

One of the reasons we fail to forgive is that we're afraid to let someone off the hook. We feel that if we don't hold on to the hurt and hold it against them, they'll get away with something. Our sense of justice demands that we hold people accountable for their infractions against us. But the problem, as we've seen, is that when we don't let people off the hook, it's WE who are hooked! We're now tied to and perhaps in bondage to the hurt for years in some cases.

But this is so unnecessary.

Why? Notice Romans 12:19—

> *Dear friends, never take revenge. Leave that to the righteous anger of God. For the Scriptures say, "I will take revenge; I will pay them back," says the LORD.*

So here's the practical reality question of the day: Who is more capable of exercising justice towards those who are guilty and unrepentant—you or God? The answer is obvious, yet I think we are sometimes unwilling to trust God in this.

The reasons for not trusting God to execute justice come back to a misunderstanding of His nature. In this case, it normally means we misunderstand His mercy. "God is too easy on people," we think. "All they have to do is pray and He'll just look the other way and let them get away with murder!"

But is that true?

Is God some kind of cosmic push-over? No! Still, I love to respond to people who get overly worked-up on this. "I WANT JUSTICE!" they'll scream. "No you don't!" I respond. "Justice means you and I go to Hell. Thank God you're not getting justice yourself!"

God will and does deliver intense and just punishment to sinners who refuse to repent and receive the sacrifice of Christ. Hell and all its agony is a reasonable response to those who destroy others with no remorse or willingness to seek Jesus to change. Jesus himself talked about Hell more than any other Biblical figure. He knew it was important to describe and reinforce the just wrath and response of Almighty God.

But even in cases where someone makes a "deathbed repentance" regarding a horrific crime, God's justice rules. What do I mean? The agony Jesus suffered in His scourging and crucifixion meant that He took the responsibility and the punishment for all horrific crimes. A truly repentant person knows this. He/she feels the overwhelming weight of sin and then the joy and release of understanding that Jesus has already paid for it. A true conversion isn't just a cop-out or an easy fix. It's an intense commitment to repent accompanied by a powerful relief based on grace. It's a realization the justice HAS been executed. Sin wasn't "overlooked." Nobody was "let off the hook." No—Jesus just stepped in and took the beating, shed his blood, and died to fulfill justice for all!

The Old Testament prophet Jonah was challenged with his view of God when asked to preach repentance to the leaders of Nineveh. The capital city of Israel's greatest enemy nation, Nineveh would be spared if they turned to God and Jonah knew it. The book ends with him pouting in anger over God's decision to extend mercy to the people and livestock of Nineveh after they turned to God with fasting and prayer (Jonah 4:10-11).

How absurd! If our enemy repents, this is good! If he/she doesn't, God is good! It's a win/win reality if we put our faith in God's judgment and His justice.

So my friends, our forgiveness is necessary because it gets us out of the way. It sets us free, and it acknowledges God as the ONLY one capable of discerning the appropriate response to the guilty. Quite frankly, He will do this anyway, but it may speed the process. Forgiveness also removes the mirage of our involvement and relieves our bitterness, anger, resentment, etc. When we fail to obey God by forgiving others, it "muddies the waters" of justice in our minds and the minds of others. It creates openings in the spiritual realm for demonic attack. It distracts from the true source of the original problem—the sin of the one who hurt us. God should be the sole source of retribution. Either He will give them the most devastating penalty imaginable in Hell or, He will take their penalty on His own back because they have truly turned away in remorse and have put their trust in his mercy.

You and I aren't able to make that determination! We can't know the hearts of our abusers. We only know what happened—we can't see what, if anything, may have changed. Or, even if they are great actors and seem to have turned their lives around, we can't see the true reality of their ugly, rock-hard hearts.

But God can. Notice—

"The human heart is the most deceitful of all things, and desperately wicked. Who really knows how bad it is? ¹⁰ But I, the LORD, search all hearts and examine secret motives. I give all people their due rewards, according to what their actions deserve (Jer. 17:9-10)."

So get out of the way. Exercise the necessity of forgiveness and trust God to take it from there. Only He is faithful enough, wise enough, and just enough to respond.

Then, you can get on with your life. Forgiveness allows a fresh start...more on that in chapter thirteen.

Chapter Thirteen: Forgiveness IS a Beginning

When we forgive, we are truly free. We're free from the chains and burdens of the past. We are thus free to start over. This means great things for us, for those we love, and yes, it may mean great things for the ones we've forgiven as well.

We've all heard stories of criminals, even murderers, who have been forgiven by those most devastated by their crimes. Sometimes, this literally turns those criminals into Christians. They repent. They surrender to the grace of Christ. And, they are transformed. This not only means good things for them, it means a powerful witness to other inmates, their family members, etc.

But nowhere is forgiveness more powerful as a fresh start than in marriage. I've counseled and worked with couples for more than a quarter century. I've seen some awesome miraculous relationship transformations. Sadly, I've seen others where bitterness and unforgiveness has killed a marriage and devastated a family.

In an earlier chapter, we talked about how forgiveness is not the same as reconciliation. I can't stress the importance of this distinction enough! Still, while separate, the two are related in that true reconciliation can't occur without forgiveness. If one or both partners in a marriage refuse to forgive, the marriage is doomed. Even if the guilty party (or, more commonly, part-ies) repent, if there's no forgiveness, there will be no healing.

What good does it do to withhold forgiveness in light of what we've studied together thus far? How does it help us? How does it help our spouse or others? How does it honor and allow intimacy with God?

It doesn't—period! It just doesn't!

For those struggling with this, I recommend not only Dr. Neil Anderson's material mentioned earlier, but also the "Prepare-Enrich" couples program created by Life Innovations, Inc.[2] Prepare-Enrich is a couple's inventory used by hundreds of thousands of couples around the world to identify relationship strengths and weaknesses. It also allows pastors and counselors to facilitate multiple exercises to build communication, conflict resolution, parenting, and other relationship skills.

In the accompanying workbook, Prepare-Enrich contains some helpful tools for seeking and granting forgiveness. I strongly recommend taking advantage of this. You can find out more at www.prepare-enrich.com.

This brings me to another issue. Throughout this book, I've focused on fallacies and truths regarding our need to forgive others. But what about when it's you or I who need to be forgiven?

Seeking Forgiveness From Others

I've waited until this point in the book to discuss this because I believe that until you understand forgiveness and are granting it to others on a regular basis, you're probably not ready to seek it either. If you are caught-up in one of the fallacies in the first half of this publication, you'll be seeking the wrong things. If you haven't embraced the truth of the second half of the book you may not even know what to ask for when approaching someone you've hurt.

Another question that comes up is whether or not to seek it at all? What if the person you hurt doesn't even know what you did? What if you cheated on your spouse years ago or you took money from your friend's wallet? When do you tell them and ask for forgiveness and when do you just give it to God (forgiving yourself) and move on?

I don't mean to suggest a glib, simple answer, but the principle at work is, love. If you seeking forgiveness will help the other person—do it! If it will simply hurt them by revealing something they don't need to know, don't. In that case, and frankly in all cases, God's forgiveness is sufficient for you.

Yet, when you know you've hurt someone and there's a rift in the relationship—you need to ask them to forgive by turning you and what you did/didn't do, over to God. Even if you know they are unlikely to let it go, asking them to do so may help them move forward in the long run.

What if they're mad, but you believe you're innocent? Our understanding of forgiveness makes it clear that seeking forgiveness is STILL the right thing to do. Remember that whether the infraction is real, imagined, or some combination thereof, the BEST thing for them to do is to turn it over to God. This is also the best for your relationship since unless he/she forgives, no real reconciliation and healing can occur.

"What?" you may ask, "You want me to apologize for something I didn't do?" No. That's not the answer. Still, you CAN apologize for the rift in your relationship (even if it WASN'T your fault), by saying, "I'm sorry that we've had this falling-out and for anything I did that might have hurt you." Is this true? Of course it is, even if you believe you're innocent. What you're really seeking is for them to let it go and move on—God's way. This is right and wise.

And, once forgiveness occurs, you can "hit the reset button." It's a new start. Now you can carefully, patiently, lovingly build on the solid foundation of the sacrifice of Jesus and the truth of His Word.

Chapter Fourteen: Conclusion....

So we've looked at what forgiveness is…and what it isn't. We've hopefully dispelled several myths and left you with the simple truth of what forgiveness really entails based on the cross of Christ.

So now what?

If you've never done so, I strongly recommend you process the "Steps to Freedom in Christ." Dr. Neil Andersons' books "The Bondage Breaker" and "Victory Over Darkness" would be great next steps in preparation. If we can help, you can contact CT Community Freedom Ministry at 860-680-7567. My wife Karen runs this ministry and would be happy to guide you through this important option.

I think the most important thing regarding forgiveness is the Nike slogan—Just Do It! Once you've cleared the cobwebs of false ideas regarding forgiveness and gained some clarity on what God says it actually is, the key is to get alone somewhere, pray for help in identifying those you need to forgive, and literally give them to God using the prayer we outlined in Chapter Nine.

Our prayer for you is that you'll be free by setting those who have hurt you free to be judged by God alone. The result will be the best possible outcome for all concerned.

To that end,

Pastor Joel

Endnotes

[1] Anderson, Dr. Neil T., "Steps to Freedom in Christ."2017, Bethany House Publishers

[2] Olson, Dr. David, "Prepare-Enrich, Inc.," 1980, www.prepare-enrich.com."

About the Author

Pastor Joel L. Rissinger is the Executive Pastor at LifeWay Church in Newington, CT; the President of the Rissinger Resource Group, and a certified speaker and coach with the John Maxwell Group. More importantly, he has been married to Karen Rissinger, for 34 years. Together, they have two adult children, an awesome son-in-law, and two beautiful granddaughters, Aadi and Bryn Figueroa.

Pastor Joel started his career as a Management Consultant to companies like Johnson & Johnson, Eastman Kodak, and Saft Battery where he did personality assessment, motivational assessment, outplacement counseling, and recruiting. He also served for several years as a Marketing Executive, consulting and providing information technology solutions to companies like Bell Aerospace, Xerox, Kodak, Marriott Corporation, the State of CT, and Welch Foods.

Since 1992, Pastor Joel has been in vocational ministry, but has kept his hand in business as well. Joel has been ordained by Converge USA, as well as two other organizations. In this capacity, he has led several congregations through major transitions prior to planting Mill Pond Church in 2007 which merged with another church whose pastor he had coached, to form LifeWay in 2017. In addition, Joel has served as the Director of Church Multiplication for Converge Northeast, the New England Regional Coordinator for The Antioch School of Leadership Development, Seminar Presenter for Life Innovations, Inc., an officer and board member for the Newington Rotary, and as a Chaplain for several local companies.

Pastor Joel has been a regular speaker at the Northeast Regional Iron Sharpens Iron Conferences, the Liberty University Church Planting Emphasis Week, the Newington, CT Chamber of Commerce meetings, numerous Rotary Clubs, the CT Better Business Bureau, and other venues. In addition to his Maxwell Team certification, Joel is a graduate of the Bill Gove Speech Workshop. He has a BA in theology from Ambassador University, and MAs in both religion and religious education from Liberty University. He is the author of several books including *The Crucified Church, The Crucified Couple, Communicate to Lead, Walking to and With Jesus, and Whole 4 Life.*

To connect with Joel, visit his website, www.rissingerresourcegroup.com or call 860-500-7163.

Made in the USA
Monee, IL
02 November 2021